CATSCRIPT

Also by Marie Angel

Cottage Flowers (Pelham)
Painting for Calligraphers (Pelham/Overlook Press)
The Art of Calligraphy (Robert Hale/Scribners)
and illustrations for:
Bird, Beast and Flowers (Chatto & Windus/David Godine)
The Tale of Tuppenny by Beatrix Potter (Warne)
The Tale of the Faithful Dove by Beatrix Potter (Warne)

CATSCRIPT

MARIE ANGEL

PELHAM

PINXIT ANGEL 1973

First published in Great Britain by Pelham Books Ltd
27 Wrights Lane, London W8 5TZ
1984
Reprinted 1987

British Library Cataloguing in Publication Data
Catscript.
   1. Cats – Poetry
   2. English
   I. Angel, Marie
   831'.008'036   PR1195.C45
ISBN 0 7207 1559 8

Printed in Italy by New Interlitho Ltd, Milan

CONTENTS

ACKNOWLEDGEMENTS

For permission to use copyright poems I am grateful to the following: Sidgwick and Jackson Ltd for 'Bunch – a cat' by Claude Colleer Abbott; 'Cat' © Oxford University Press 1975: reprinted from *Other Exiles* by Edward Kamau Braithwaite (1975) by permission of Oxford University Press; Macmillan, London and Basingstoke for 'The Prayer of the Cat' from *Prayers from the Ark* by Carmen Bernos de Gasztold, translated by Rumer Godden; Faber and Faber Ltd for 'The Naming of Cats' from *Old Possum's Book of Practical Cats* by T.S. Eliot; Constable Ltd for 'Pangur Bán' from *Poems and Translations* by Robin Flower; Laurence Pollinger Ltd and the Estate of Mrs Frieda Lawrence Ravagli for 'Pax' from *The Collected Poems of D. H. Lawrence;* the Literary Trustees of Walter de la Mare, and the Society of Authors as their representative for 'Double Dutch' by Walter de la Mare; Faber and Faber Ltd for 'the old trouper' from *archy and mehitabel* by Don Marquis; the author for 'The Cat' by Robin Skelton from *Third Day Lucky* published by Oxford University Press; James MacGibbon, the Executor of the Estate of Stevie Smith for 'My Cat Major' and 'The Galloping Cat' from *The Collected Poems of Stevie Smith* published by Allen Lane The Penguin Press; Hubert Nicholson for 'Cats' by A.S.J. Tessimond; Michael Yeats and Macmillan London Ltd for 'The Cat and the Moon' from *The Collected Poems* of W.B. Yeats. The illustration on page 37 was first reproduced as a card by The Green Tiger Press. Every effort has been made to trace copyright owners, but regretfully not in every instance with success.

I would also like to thank Peter Hutchings for photographing some of my paintings (pages 2, 7, 12, 20, 21, 28, 33, 41, 53 and 56).

FOREWORD

Cats have always been as much part of my life as painting and calligraphy, and so I have a special affection for *Pangur Bán,* that poem written in the eighth century in the margins of a manuscript of St Paul's Epistles by an unknown Irish scholar about Pangur, his white cat: the friend who shared the solitude of his cell as my favourite Abyssinian cat, Ben, shares my workroom with me.

This is very much a personal anthology. The poems are some of the many that I have collected in my commonplace book over the years, as are some of the sketches, and all the miniature portraits are of my own cats.

Catscript is also a personal anthology in that many of the poets are writing about their own cats – Claude Colleer Abbott, Hal Summers, Joachim du Bellay, and poor Christopher Smart in Bedlam. Common to all is a love and respect for that most beautiful of creatures, the cat.

M·A

To Dorothy, with love

BUNCH – A CAT

I OPENED a book
And on the white glossed page
   Are the two brown pad prints
         You made.

      Down the garden path
   I watch the delicate tread
Of your feathered feet round the little bright pools
         And your questioning head;
         I see your body sweep
   Up the trunk and along the green boughs
         Of the apple trees,
      Then a clawed pad dip to thrust
At the hand that gently shakes a branch beneath
         And your beating, swaying brush.

   And still with shivering desire you creep
Where angry sparrows shrill battle in the peas,
      Where the fledgling thrushes hide,
Or the bold chaffinch tempts with frantic cheep and chide
      From his nesting mate in the elder tree.
A hundred times in vain you poise, you leap;
         Crestfallen, stand denied.
      Yet too often a broken body hangs
      Limp, in your tiger fangs.
Or you stalk, ever near and nearer,
White butterflies that flit in the sun

From sweet alyssum to fragrant phlox,
From crimson snap-dragons to lofty hollyhocks;
   And the warm dusk June nights every one
You lie deep hid in the mowing grass
Till the little white moths float crazily by
     And you follow running, leaping high.

      After milk is lapped
  By the winter fireside, on the rug,
And the dangling hare's foot tempts to no game
     On my knees you settle snug,
      Warm bunch of sweet-smelling fur,
And with rushing wind, clock tick, rustle of flame
     Drowses your sing-song purr.

You'll not come again
In your dear imperious way
To drum at the window pane
    On a rainy day;
  Never bite, clutch, kick
The hand a small rough tongue would after lick;
     No wind shall stir
  That soft luxuriance, your tawny fur;
  In your Spring, in your body's pride,
  Jet, amber, red-brown coated, agate-eyed,
    We found you in your form,
    Curled in your wonted bed
      Asleep and warm,
       But dead.   Claude Colleer Abbott

THE PRAYER OF THE CAT

Lord,
I am the cat.
It is not, exactly, that I have something to ask of You!
No –
I ask nothing of anyone –
but,
if You have by some chance, in some celestial barn,
a little white mouse,
or a saucer of milk,
I know someone who would relish them.
Wouldn't You like someday
to put a curse on the whole race of dogs?
If so I should say,

AMEN

Carmen Bernos de Gasztold
Translated from the French by Rumer Godden

MY CAT MAJOR

Major is a fine cat
What is he at?
He hunts birds in the hydrangea
And in the tree
Major was ever a ranger
He ranges where no one can see.

Sometimes he goes up to the attic
With a hooped back
His paws hit the iron rungs
Of the ladder in a quick kick
How can this be done?
It is a knack.

Oh Major is a fine cat
He walks cleverly
And what is he at, my fine cat?
No one can see.

Stevie Smith

FOR I WILL CONSIDER MY CAT JEOFFRY

For I will consider my Cat Jeoffry.

For he is the servant of the Living God, duly and daily serving him.

For he keeps the Lord's watch in the night against the adversary.

For he counteracts the powers of darkness by his electrical skin & glaring eyes.

For he counteracts the Devil, who is death, by brisking about the life.

For in his morning orisons he loves the sun and the sun loves him.

For he is of the tribe of Tiger.

For the Cherub Cat is a term of the Angel Tiger.

For he has the subtlety and hissing of a serpent, which in goodness he suppresses.

For he will not do destruction, if he is well-fed, neither will he spit without provocation.

For he purrs in thankfulness, when God tells him he's a good Cat.

from Jubilate Agno by Christopher Smart

THE NAMING OF CATS

The Naming of Cats is a difficult matter,
    It isn't just one of your holiday games;
You may think at first I'm as mad as a hatter
When I tell you, a cat must have THREE DIFFERENT NAMES.
First of all, there's the name that the family use daily,
    Such as Peter, Augustus, Alonzo or James,
Such as Victor or Jonathan, George or Bill Bailey –
    All of them sensible everyday names.
There are fancier names if you think they sound sweeter,
    Some for the gentlemen, some for the dames:
Such as Plato, Admetus, Electra, Demeter –
    But all of them sensible everyday names.
But I tell you, a cat needs a name that's particular,
    A name that's peculiar, and more dignified,
Else how can he keep up his tail perpendicular,
    Or spread out his whiskers, or cherish his pride?
Of names of this kind, I can give you a quorum,
    Such as Munkustrap, Quaxo, or Coricopat,
Such as Bombalurina, or else Jellylorum –
    Names that never belong to more than one cat.
But above and beyond there's still one name left over,
    And that is the name that you never will guess;
The name that no human research can discover –
    But THE CAT HIMSELF KNOWS, and will never confess.

When you notice a cat in profound meditation,
    The reason, I tell you, is always the same:
His mind is engaged in a rapt contemplation
    Of the thought, of the thought, of the thought of his name:
        His ineffable effable
        Effanineffable
Deep and inscrutable singular Name.

T.S. Eliot

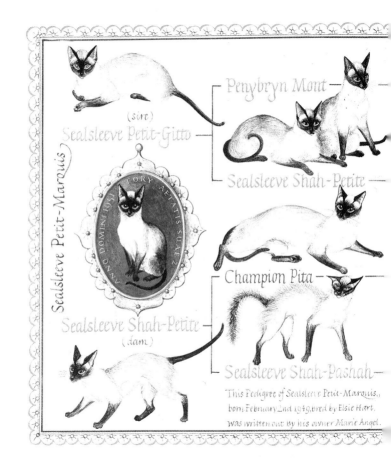

Penybryn Mont

(sire)
Sealsleeve Petit-Gitto

Sealsleeve Shah-Petite

Sealsleeve Petit-Marquis

ANNO DOMINI 1951 · ·ORY· AETATIS SUAE 2

Champion Pita

Sealsleeve Shah-Petite
(dam)

Sealsleeve Shah-Pashah

This Pedigree of Sealsleeve Petit-Marquis,
born February 2nd 1949, bred by Elsie Hart,
was written out by his owner Marie Angel.

- Penybryn Llin
- Longham Raguya

Champion Pita

- Sealsleeve Shah-Pashah

- Southampton Jupiter

- Aouda

- Oriental Silky Boy

- Dromore Biru

- Celesto
- Longham Raguya
- Leprecaun
- Slingsby Beryl
- Southampton Jupiter
- Aouda
- Oriental Silky Boy
- Dromore Biru
- Champion Kitya Nama
- Southampton Lucinda
- Prestwick Puteh Punya
- Champion Simzette
- Champion Angus Silky
- Sirius Valentina
- Champion Prestwick Mata-Biru
- Dromore Souriya

THE CAT

The cat stood under the lilac.
It was black.
The sky was blue, the grass green,
and it stood
black under the lilac
that was lilac
under the sky that was all over blue.

No matter that the way we say is how
the thing is in the mind, a proof of sorts
that where we stand and look is what we are,
sometimes a black cat stands black under lilac
and the grass is green, the sky unknown.

Robin Skelton

THE GALLOPING CAT

Oh I am a cat that likes to
Gallop about doing good
So
One day when I was
Galloping about doing good, I saw
A Figure in the path; I said:
Get off! (Be-
cause
I am a cat that likes to
Gallop about doing good)
But he did not move, instead
He raised his hand as if
To land me a cuff

24

So I made to dodge so as to
Prevent him bring it orf,
Un-for-tune-ately I slid
On a banana skin
Some Ass had left instead
Of putting in the bin. So
His hand caught me on the cheek
I tried
To lay his arm open from wrist to elbow
With my sharp teeth
Because I am
A cat that likes to gallop about doing good.
Would you believe it?
He wasn't there
My teeth met nothing but air,
But a Voice said: Poor cat,
(Meaning me) and a soft stroke
Came on me head
Since when
I have been bald.
I regard myself as
A martyr to doing good.
Also I heard a swoosh
As of wings, and saw
A halo shining at the height of
Mrs Gubbins's backyard fence,

So I thought: What's the good
Of galloping about doing good
When angels stand in the path
And do not do as they should
Such as having an arm to be bitten off
All the same I
Intend to go on being
A cat that likes to
Gallop about doing good
So
Now with my bald head I go,
Chopping the untidy flowers down, to and fro,
An' scooping up the grass to show
Underneath
The cinder path of wrath
Ha ha ha ha, ho,
Angels aren't the only ones who do not know
What's what and that
Galloping about doing good
Is a full-time job
That needs
An experienced eye of earthly
Sharpness, worth I dare say
(If you'll forgive a personal note)
A good deal more

Than all that skyey stuff
Of angels that make so bold as
To pity a cat like me that
Gallops about doing good.

Stevie Smith

27

MY OLD CAT

My old cat is dead,
Who would butt me with his head.
He had the sleekest fur.
He had the blackest purr.
Always gentle with us
Was this black puss,
But when I found him today
Stiff and cold where he lay
His look was a lion's,
Full of rage, defiance:
Oh, he would not pretend
That what came was a friend
But met it in pure hate.
Well died, my old cat.

Hal Summers

THE CAT AND THE MOON

THE cat went here and there
And the moon spun round like a top,
And the nearest kin of the moon,
The creeping cat, looked up.
Black Minnaloushe stared at the moon,
For, wander and wail as he would,
The pure cold light in the sky
Troubled his animal blood.
Minnaloushe runs in the grass
Lifting his delicate feet.
Do you dance, Minnaloushe, do you dance?
When two close kindred meet,
What better than call a dance?
Maybe the moon may learn,
Tired of that courtly fashion,
A new dance turn.
Minnaloushe creeps through the grass
From moonlit place to place,
The sacred moon overhead
Has taken a new phase.
Does Minnaloushe know that his pupils
Will pass from change to change,
And that from round to crescent,
From crescent to round they range?

Minnaloushe creeps through the grass
Alone, important and wise,
And lifts to the changing moon
His changing eyes.

W.B. Yeats

CAT

To plan plan to create to have
whiskers cool carat silver ready and curved
bristling

to plan plan to create to have
eyes green doors that dilate greenest
pouncers

to be ready rubber ball ready
feet bouncers cool fluid in
tension

to be steady steady claws all
attention to wait wait and create
pouncing

to be a cat eeling through alleys
slipping through windows of odours
to feel swiftness slowly

to halt at the gate hearing
unlocking whispers paper feet wrapping
potatoes and papers

to hear nicely mice spider feet
scratching great horny nails
catching a fire flies wire legs etch-

ing yet stretching beyond this arch
untriumphant lazily rubb-
ing the soft fur of home

Edward Brathwaite

POEM

As the cat
climbed over
the top of

the jamcloset
first the right
forefoot

carefully
then the hind
stepped down

into the pit of
the empty
flowerpot

William Carlos Williams

PAX

ALL that matters is to be at one with the living God
to be a creature in the house of the God of Life.

Like a cat asleep on a chair
at peace, in peace
and at one with the master of the house, with the mistress,
at home, at home in the house of the living,
sleeping on the hearth, and yawning before the fire.

Sleeping on the hearth of the living world
yawning at home before the fire of life
feeling the presence of the living God
like a great reassurance
a deep calm in the heart
a presence
as of the master sitting at the board
in his own greater being,
in the house of life.

D.H. Lawrence

ALL THAT MATTERS
is to be at one with the living GOD
To be a creature in the house of the
GOD OF LIFE.

Like a cat asleep on a chair
At peace, in peace
And at one with the master
of the house, with the mistress,
AT HOME...

THE OLD TROUPER

i ran onto mehitabel again
last evening
she is inhabiting
a decayed trunk
which lies in an alley
in greenwich village
in company with the
most villainous tom cat
i have ever seen
it is a theatre trunk
archy mehitabel told me
and tom is an old theatre cat
he has given his life
to the theatre
the stage is not what it
used to be tom says
he puts his front paw
on his breast and says
they don t have it any more
they don t have it here
the old troupers are gone
there s nobody can troupe
any more
they are all amateurs nowadays

they haven t got it
here
there are only
five or six of us oldtime
troupers left
my grandfather
was with forrest
he had it he was a real trouper
my grandfather said
he had a voice
that used to shake
the ferry boats
on the north river
once he lost his beard
and my grandfather
dropped from the
fly gallery and landed
under his chin
and played his beard
for the rest of the act
you don t see any theatre
cats that could do that
nowadays
they haven t got it they
haven t got it
here

39

once i played the owl
in modjeska s production
of macbeth
i sat above the castle gate
in the murder scene
and made my yellow
eyes shine through the dusk
like an owl s eyes
modjeska was a real
trouper she knew how to pick
her support i would like
to see any of these modern
theatre cats play the owl s eyes
to modjeska s lady macbeth
but they haven t got it nowadays
they haven t got it
here

mehitabel he says
both our professions
are being ruined
by amateurs

(Archy is a cockroach
who types his poems
on an office typewri-
ter. He is not strong
enough to work the
shift key for capital
letters.)

archy
Don Marquis (*adapted*)

LITTLE CAT

Little cat,
Little cat,
Little cat in the road!
Whose cat are you?
Whose cat are you?
Damn it, I'm my own cat.

Piet Hein
(translated from the Danish)

CATS

Cats, no less liquid than their shadows,
   Offer no angles to the wind.
They slip, diminished, neat, through loopholes
   Less than themselves; will not be pinned

To rules or routed for journeys; counter
   Attack with non-resistance; twist
Enticing through the curving fingers
   And leave an angered, empty fist.

They wait, obsequious as darkness,
   Quick to retire, quick to return;
Admit no aim or ethics; flatter
   With reservations; will not learn

To answer to their names; are seldom
   Truly owned till shot and skinned.
Cats, no less liquid than their shadows,
   Offer no angles to the wind.

A.S.J. Tessimond

PINXIT
1967 - 1970

EPITAPH ON A PET CAT · 1525 Joachim Du Bellay 1560

Belaud first let me say,
Was not entirely grey
Like cats bred here at home,
But more like those in Rome,
His fur being silver grey
And fine and smooth as satin
While lying back he'd display
A white expanse of ermine.
Small muzzle, tiny teeth;
Eyes of a tempered warmth,
Whose pupils of dark green
Showed every colour seen
In the bow which splendidly
Arches the rainy sky.

This was Belaud, a gentle
Animal, whose title
To beauty was so sure
He'd no competitor!
A sad and bitter cross!
Irreparable loss!

Belaud was well behaved
And in no way depraved;
His only ravages

Were on an ancient cheese,
A finch and a young linnet
Whose trillings seemed to get
On Belaud's nerves – but then
How perfect are we men?

God grant to me, Belaud
Command of speech to show
Your gentle nature forth
In words of fitting worth,
Your qualities to state
In verse as delicate,
That you may live while cats
Wage mortal war on rats.

Joachim du Bellay

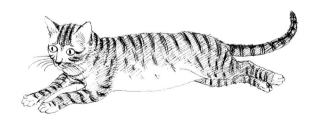

DOUBLE DUTCH

That crafty cat, a buff-black Siamese,
Sniffing through wild wood, sagely, silently goes –
Prick ears, lank legs, alertly twitching nose –
And on her secret errand reads with ease
A language no man knows.

Walter de la Mare

THE CAT

The cat beneath the chassis knows
What's best for shelter and repose,
So do not try to start your car
   Before you know how matters are.

Puss has an intense disgust
   Of being mingled in the dust,
So pray be courteous on the road –
   Let CATS be in the Highway Code.

There's nothing really very much in
   Looking, before you let your clutch in;
Such circumspection may well save
   Little Grimalkin from a grave!

Eric Clough Taylor

PANGUR BÁN

I and Pangur Bán, my cat,
'Tis a like task we are at;
Hunting mice is his delight,
Hunting words I sit all night.

Better far than praise of men
'Tis to sit with book and pen;
Pangur bears me no ill will,
He too plies his simple skill.

'Tis a merry thing to see
At our tasks how glad are we,
When at home we sit and find
Entertainment to our mind.

Oftentimes a mouse will stray
In the hero Pangur's way;
Oftentimes my keen thought set
Takes a meaning in its net.

'Gainst the wall he sets his eye
Full and fierce and sharp and sly;
'Gainst the wall of knowledge I
All my little wisdom try.

PANGUR
BAN

When a mouse darts from its den,
O how glad is Pangur then!
O what gladness do I prove
When I solve the doubts I love!

So in peace our tasks we ply,
Pangur Bán, my cat, and I;
In our arts we find our bliss,
I have mine and he has his.

Practice every day has made
Pangur perfect in his trade;
I get wisdom day and night
Turning darkness into light.

Translated by Robin Flower from
an eighth century Irish manuscript

CRUEL CLEVER CAT

Sally, having swallowed cheese,
Directs down holes the scented breeze,
Enticing thus with baited breath
Nice mice to an untimely death.

Geoffrey Taylor

CATMINT

Bear in mind
 Never to push a cat from behind;
 There is no humiliation for a cat
 Greater than that.

 Cats are proud
And no familiarity is allowed.
 To a friend
They will condescend
And occasionally are seen
 To lean;
But they will not go out of their way
 To betray
Signs of affection
Or recollection
Nor will incline their ears
 To taunts or jeers.
At the least presentiment
 Of sentiment
They simply retire
 In ire.
Do not shout or call
That would not do at all.

Fish and milk
   And that ilk
May be used as easement
   And appeasement
But even mice
Do not entice
   The well-bred,
For the cat
   Is an aristocrat;
Get that into your head.

Eric Clough Taylor

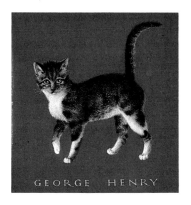

GEORGE HENRY

ON THE DEATH OF A FAVOURITE CAT

'Twas on a lofty vase's side,
Where China's gayest art had dyed
　　The azure flowers that blow,
Demurest of the tabby kind,
The pensive Selima, reclined,
　　Gazed on the lake below.

Her conscious tail her joy declared:
The fair round face, the snowy beard,
　　The velvet of her paws,
Her coat that with the tortoise vies,
Her ears of jet, and emerald eyes,
　　She saw; and purred applause.

Still had she gazed; but 'midst the tide
Two angel forms were seen to glide,
　　The genii of the stream:
Their scaly armour's Tyrian hue
Through richest purple to the view
　　Betrayed a golden gleam.

The hapless nymph with wonder saw:
A whisker first and then a claw,
　　With many an ardent wish,
She stretched, in vain, to reach the prize.
What female heart can gold despise?
　　What cat's averse to fish?

Presumptuous maid! with looks intent
Again she stretched, again she bent,
    Nor knew the gulf between.
(Malignant Fate sat by, and smiled.)
The slippery verge her feet beguiled;
    She tumbled headlong in.

From hence, ye beauties, undeceived,
Know one false step is ne'er retrieved,
    And be with caution bold:
Not all that tempts your wandering eyes
And heedless hearts is lawful prize,
    Nor all that glisters, gold.

Thomas Gray

When I play with my cat, who knows
whether she is not amusing herself more
with me than I with her.

Michel de Montaigne

SCRIPSIT

ANGEL

ET PINXIT 1958-1960